To

Jakki

thanks for the

Enjoy

Christopher

Life in Poetry

Eyes Open to the World

G.A. Christopher

authorHOUSE™
1663 Liberty Drive, Suite 200
Bloomington, Indiana 47403
(800) 839-8640
www.AuthorHouse.com

First published by AuthorHouse 09/09/05

ISBN: 1-4208-6865-9 (e)
ISBN: 1-4208-6864-0 (sc)

Printed in the United States of America
Bloomington, Indiana

This book is printed on acid-free paper.

This book is dedicated to those who have dreams and aspirations and are willing to do something about it.

G.A. Christopher

Table of Contents

A WOMAN OF WORTH

The price of a woman
Will never be defined.
How can you price someone
Who is more elegant than wine?

Through thousands of years
They shaped the earth
They have this special gift
Only they can give birth.

The love of a woman
Is more precious than gold.
We all need to be loved
Whether young or old.

A man can love a woman
With all his heart.
When a woman loves a man
It's till death do us part.

The strength of a woman
Is not how much she can lift
Because she is the nucleus
When the man goes adrift.

Every man loves a woman
We cannot deny
Without a woman to love
Our species would die.

So treat her special
Not just for a day
For true love can be found
Just a stones throw away.

As boys we grow up
Now stand tall as men
The love of a woman stops
Us going around the bend

Because Mother's Day is celebrated
All over the world
Give thanks to all women
All woman of worth.

TONI-ANN BYFIELD

TONI-ANN BYFIELD was a beautiful girl
She didn't deserve to leave this world
Just seven years old she had time on her hands
That cold-blooded assassin
Just didn't give a damn
He shot her in the back
Like the assassin he is
It makes me feel angry from way down within
It could have been my cousin, nephew or niece
How could I depend on the so-called police?
These guys they don't care
They have no remorse
They seem to kill blacks
Like it's some kind of cause
My blood feels so hot
I have to cool down
The tears in my eyes
Though she wasn't my own
So young and so sweet
She couldn't fight back
That deadly assassin must have been on the crack
Man will kill man for all sorts of things
Man who kills child has the devil within
Her life had yet to start
Could have done many things
Like train to be a doctor, or learn how to sing
While writing this poem I am praying within
That somehow black people can stop the killing.

GUNS AND KNIVES

Guns and knives have no place on our streets
I wish I could reach out and maybe teach

Mothers are crying sisters are weeping
All for the love of a brother now sleeping
Was he killed by a plane or run over by a truck?
Did he fall off a ladder?
No, he was killed by a gunshot

The youths of today have no respect for life
It's all about the bling that they dream about at night

Another day another funeral all dressed in black
Another youth got killed by a stab in the back

How many parents are frightened when their kids go to school
When knives replace fists as the local tool
The respect was gone when we called our sisters ho's
The respect was gone when we left our kids alone
No one to guide them no father figure at home
The streets are their life, will kill for a mobile phone

A gun has no feelings a gun has no brains
A gun does not choose who you blow away
Another got killed as he sat in his car
No witness around no witness by far

Every week there's a stabbing or someone being shot
We should all take a look at the problem we got

Get rid of the crack dens at least it's a start
There must be a way to keep these young gangs apart

Through the videos that they watch
And the music that they hear
They will never afford the bling
That their role models wear

It's time for education
It's time they saw the light
Their lives will never move forward
If they choose to run and fight.

CIGARETTES

That little white stick
Which you hold in your mouth
Have so many diseases that affect your health
It's hard to give up
Ask someone who smokes
If you say they're addicted
They will say you're a joke

There are warnings on the boxes
Warning you of death
From Bensons to Superkings
Some like passive smoke instead
They say that smoking kills
As it eats away at your cells

The Government has put the price up again
Some people can't pay their bills
The cancer is like an agent
It will seek you out one day
The cravings are hard to put into words
But can take your breath away

Some kids are starting young
As they smoke throughout the day
Their clothes are kinda smelly
And their teeth brown with decay

The smoke affects your taste buds
As you add a little salt
Fish fingers used to taste so good
Until you started to smoke

We have to address the problem
And we have to address it now
Ban smoking from pubs and restaurants
Ban smoking from the inner towns
No smoking for the under 18's
Though they may not thank us now

But when they grow into adulthood
Their lungs will be clear and sound.

LONDON TOWN

Whenever in London Town
You must visit the Queen
At home in Buckingham Palace
Where she lives tax-free.
From Marble Arch to Park Lane
There's so much you can do
Regents Park is home to London Zoo,
Millennium wheel on the South Bank
Big Ben on the North
The Tower of London in the East
Up the road from Canary Wharf,
Then the trips on the Thames
For a different kind of view
Shopping in Oxford Street
For the likes of me and you.
Take a bus or a black cab
Regulated by The Mayor
You won't get so ripped off
By the cowboys out there,
Covent Garden for the opera fans
Have a break in Leicester Square
Theatergoers on Shaftsbury Avenue
Bow ties and frocks with flairs,
Have you heard of Sherlock Holmes
Who lived on Baker Street?
Madam Tussauds round the corner
With dummies that look so neat.
Kings Cross and Euston Stations
They're not so far away
Take a trip on the Underground
Where the trains run all day
Whitehall the centre of Government
In Downing Street lives the Blair's
Trafalgar Square just up the road

Tate Gallery with paintings so rare
Don't forget the Harrods store
Where the rich and famous go
Scotland Yard on Victoria Street
The Chinese live in Soho
Kensington Palace where Diana lived
There's a memorial shaped like a moat
In Hyde Park you can have a snack
Or take a ride on a boat.

BULLIES

Bullies are truly cowards
From the gutters they will rise
Their victims are nothing more than a notch
They're not even worth a prize

The secret of a bully is to find somebody weak
They haven't the words to manipulate
So they use their hands and feet

The victims are affected in so many little ways
Through emotional stress
And living in fear
Some hide from school in fear

No need to suffer in silence
Because we know it's not your fault
You're not alone there's kids like you
All to young to vote

Some look over their shoulders
As they go to school
Their money their sweets
Some even lose their shoes

It's the start of anti-bullying week
And it starts all over this land
Bullies who make life a misery
Should automatically receive a ban

Backed by the stars like Thierry Henri
The world has opened its eyes
For it's time to end the bully season
Let the children get on with their lives

Some haven't the strength to fight back
Some can't and even won't
Help is at hand
Dial the Child Line
Wear the blue band of hope

NIGHT THOUGHTS

There's a shadow in the street
Over sixteen feet high
That street lamp stands out
In the middle of the night
Tjan and Shirley are now fast asleep
The TV is on
Radiator glows with heat
I've got this writing bug
That I can't let go
The view from this window
Wouldn't you like to know?
It's a mystery how we evolved
And the time we got left
It's hard to imagine life after death
Though the tears will run dry
But the feelings live on
Have visions of this planet
Looking like a mushroom
Played soldiers as a kid
But now I am a man
Still searching for that something
That puts me in demand
The heaven and The Father
Infinity and in space
Is Mars a place for all of us
Or destined for one race?
The thoughts that bounce around my head

If only I could make be real
I would float in space
Look back at Earth
Give every one a free meal
Shadows come and go
Like thieves in the night
The soul can be a lonely place
When the brains not thinking right
Give thanks to those around us
Who believe in what we can do
It's up to us to move ahead
Believe in something called
YOU.

CARNIVAL TIME

The music so crisp
The whistle so clear
It's that time again
For the carnival fair

Floats and bands
Bright costumes too
Please don't come with your
Tight fitting shoes

People laughing and singing aloud
Forget all your worries
Come join the crowd
Taste good food from
All over the world
Like spicy jerk chicken
From that Caribbean girl

Sounds Systems playing on every street
From Reggae to Soca
To that Hip Hop beat
As the base thumps your chest
And the treble rings your ears
Lots of wine flowing
Me? I'm drinking my beers

First started in Grove
W10 if you don't know
By the West Indian immigrants
Over thirty-eight years ago

Only had a few drums
Way back then
But look at it now
It's bigger than Big Ben

But it goes back further to 1835
When slavery was abolished
And the people came alive
They began dancing in the streets
And poured scorn on the system
That enslaved them for so long

It's the largest festival in Europe
The biggest so far
Two million people dancing
Through Westbourne Park

Live shows in the evening
How good can it get?
Black and white together
Working up a sweat.

WAR ON TERROR

You see what you see
But it isn't all what it seems
We have enemies amongst us
Who live to deceive

And though their rewards lie high above
They create havoc among people we love

The enemy's not us
But the people in charge
But we're in the front line
So give us a mask

You lie fifty feet down protected by rocks
We lie upper ground
Dying in our socks

And now the banks will quash our debts
For there is no man to come and collect
Although the masks are selling fast
A hundred pounds is a bit of a farce

The Government boys get theirs for free
Along with a bunker, cookies and tea
It has no colour taste or smell
But apparently so it will send you to hell

But if you've been lucky and had a jab
I hear the effects isn't too bad
It's better than choking and dying real slow
I hope it's not real
I have nowhere to go

But if you are lucky
And know a man
Who knows a man
You too can be saved
From the one called Saddam.

AFTER IRAQ

The country's in fear
The world is in fear
What kind of bomb, be fired
From North Korea?

Don't panic
Don't fear
The end will come fast
You won't even feel the initial blast

Devastation will be mighty
Like a flash in the night
Not even dark glasses will save your sight

Mushroom clouds growing
Sucking the air
What kind of effects on the atmosphere?

Half of the planet
Covered in dust
No human beings,
Just nuclear musk

Those that survived
Could have come from Star Trek
With heads on their feet
And toes on their back

Those in their bunkers
Were saved from the effects
We couldn't be saved
Though we wore nuclear vest

Like watching TV
And seeing it unfold
Like being in a drama
I never was told

If the Japs' have started the term 'Doomsday'
What military hardware
Will the Americans display?

The effects will be big
The bang so loud
Even from Mars
You will see a cloud

The US will be hit
And the English too
Who will be left standing?
I'll leave it to you.

A CROSS TO BARE

People come and go in our lives
Sometimes without thought or even feelings
We all have a cross to bare within
Because we're just human beings

Some people touch our hearts and minds
While others will leave us seething
The objective in life is to be at peace with oneself
All liars and deceivers have no meaning

We can't be something then preach to be another
Because that is the art of deceiving
The way we get used and sometimes abused
Just prove they have no feelings

Have to be strong bring no emotions along
If shown will be broken and weaken
We all have a heart that sets us apart
But there's those who's hearts are freezing

They have shown to be cold right down to the bone
So it's time you thought about leaving
Forgive and forget is the way to move on
Air in your lungs is for breathing

Don't let the past put a mist in your path
For it's time to get over the grieving
Through the people we meet we can all take one thing
Thank goodness we're all God's children.

THE COLOUR BLACK

Have you ever read a book that's not written in black?
This is not fiction but a natural fact
Black armbands are worn to remember the dead
Black coffee is drunk to keep you up till ten

Black is a colour that has good and bad
Like blackmail and black mark but it's not all sad

Have you ever seen a black sheep?
And been called one yourself?
Just been to an air-show saw a plane they call Stealth

Hailed a black cab while in the West End
Ate some black pudding with my sister's boyfriend

Can you remember at school when the blackboards where black
And the trips to Blackpool made us want to go back

Black hole and black space is what Astronauts see
Black Book is what I look in to find a date for me

Have you been to the Caribbean and tried black-eyed peas?
Had a friend who done boxing and got a black eye for free?

Black polish on my shoes some put it on their face
When confronted by the enemy they can't tell their true race

Have you been to the bank and been told you're 'in the black'?
Woke up one night and saw my shadow look back

Have you ever seen a car where the tyres are not black?
There is a division in London that fights black on black

Black nails is what you get if you don't keep them clean
Black market is where you go to get that cheap washing machine

Only wear a black suit to see off the dead
Some people only go to the wake instead

It's called a 'black day' when things go so wrong
In prison there is a black room where they keep all the cons

Just remember that black isn't all about bad
You can have a red mist that can turn you real mad

DAVID BLAINE

Why does this man choose
To show us his pain?
That man in a glass box
They call David BLAINE
He used to do card tricks
Which was shown on TV
He stood in an icebox at minus degrees
He stood on a pole
For over fourteen days
This man David Blaine
Ceases to amaze
This thing about starvation
I can't comprehend
When it's done for real
With no fee at the end
He may have lost four stones
But gained three million
What about those people
With starving children?
There's people in the Third World
That does this for free
With no TV cameras
Or water that's clean
What about the people
Who are starving for real
Is this to show it's no big deal?
To go without food for forty four days
Is this man for real?
Or is he starting a craze?
David Blaine is a great illusionist
But this time round
I think he's just using us
As he hangs over the Thames
People watch in suspense
Will this great magician
Make it till the end?

THE HI-VI VEST

A Hi-Vi Vest is not good in your bag
It must be worn
When you enter Metro Land

When walking between buses
You know you have to be seen
Or you could end up like
A TV with a plasma screen

A Hi-Vi Vest is so light and bright
You can even be seen
In the middle of the night

Wearing a Hi-Vi Vest isn't all that bad
It's lighter than the sandwiches
You carry in your bag

A Hi-Vi Vest is free to all
It comes in all sizes
For the fat, thin and tall

So make no bones
There's one that can fit
If seen at work without it
You're in for some stick

A Hi-Vi Vest must be worn on your back
Not carried in your hand
Like you're carrying a snack

No good around your waist
Like you're wearing a belt
If you happen to get hit
Do you think the Union would help?

It is not a form of punishment
It could save your life
So make the Manager happy
Always wear it when on site.

HYDE PARK

Whenever in London
You must visit Hyde Park
Don't go there too late
It closes after dark
At the top of Oxford Street
And next to Park Lane
Marble Arch is just a stones throw away
With its acres of green
And horse riding tracks
There are plenty of places
You can stop for a snack
Music being played all over the park
Some people play fighting
Just having a laugh
The centre of attraction
Is the Serpentine Lake
Where it's stood for years
Seen Prince's and Sheik's
You can hire a boat
For an hour or two
Or paddle with the one who's close to you
You can go for a swim
In the heat of the day
Where the kids can have fun
In a safe place to play
Skate boarders and cyclists
Mingle as one
Couples holding hands
While strolling in the sun
There's a place called Speaker's Corner
Where you go and have your say
About politics or religion
You choose the topic of the day
There's ducks and swans
For the kids to see
Throwing breadcrumbs
For the birds to eat
No vans or trucks

Are allowed in the park
But there's always one
Who will take a chance
Ice cream and burgers
Washed down with some squash
In the morning catch the stars
As they go for a jog
So bring on the sun
And head to the park
It's free entertainment
And free for your car

THE ROUTE MASTER

I'm gonna miss that old Bus
With no doors at the end
That Route Master model
We knew as a friend

The sound of the engine
As it chugs through the streets
Sometimes find chewing gum
Stuck to the seats

Used to hang off the pole
With feet in the air
30mph with the wind in my hair

As the smoke spits out
While stuck in a jam
Tourists taking pictures
Some end up in Japan

An Icon in London for over fifty odd years
Only Buckingham Palace
Can raise more tears

In winter they were cold
And in summer they were hot
They were made of aluminum
At least they won't rot

Big Bendy Busses
Now champions of the streets
Followed by T.P's and V.P's in
This ever-changing fleet

Route Masters being sold off
To the likes of you and me
Sixty-four seats up for grabs
For those friends and families

They were cheap to insure
With the mileage to the moon
Watch out for low bridges
Might see some converted soon!

CHANGING TIMES

When as a young man
We fought with our fists
The odd knife was shown
But we all knew the risks

The fighting would last
For minutes no end
All battered and bruised
We fought for a friend

But in the end we could all walk home
A busted eye and my best clothes torn
His lips was busted
Nose bent to the right
But other than that
He would live to fight

But nowadays the fighting's all changed
Some think they're assassins
They think it's a game

Some of the guys are killed for their clothes
Some of them killed for the way that they pose
And though we wish the killings would stop
We pray for the price of Reeboks to drop

At first it was stabbings
But now it's the gun
How did all this violence really begin?

And now its time to hold a truce
'Cos you could be caught
In the cross fire noose

What used to be fist
Has turned into gun
I remember when fighting used to be fun

S.A.R.S

They say that diseases come and go
Remember The Plague
I told you so
In 1918 they had the Spanish Flu
It killed more people than World War II

Then came AIDS, it killed much more
In Africa, England and Singapore
But now we have a modern-day plague
It's a disease called S.A.R.S.
I'm afraid to say

It spreads much faster than AIDS and the Flu
They say you can catch it by flushing the loo

It sits in the air when coughed or sneezed
The first fatality brought the Welsh to their knees
The W.H.O. says not to panic
Only 5% die, that's not being pragmatic

Spitting in public has been banned in Hong Kong
We cannot say if this is right or wrong
People wear facemasks to protect themselves
Afraid of the dangers causing havoc among cells

The symptoms are clear we have to watch out
Like the rise in your temperature, can't breath or shout
You may be quarantined for over ten days
Six hundred cases worldwide
I'm sad to say

Schools are shut people stay at home
If a man sneezes next to you
Just leave him alone

Just one thing to say, it's not all doom and gloom
Cancer and heart disease kills more than the flu

THE COLOUR WHITE

There's a White House in London
Not many people will know
Whitechapel in the East
Brick Lane a stones throw

Joe Bugner was a boxer
He was known as The Great White Hope
But got flatten so many times
His name switch to White Dope

White flag is what you wave
If you don't want to carry on
White heat is what you get
If you leave the oven on

White Paper is the one
Which the Government rubber stamps
White rose is very rare to find
White elephant and white ants

Have you ever seen a white bear
Holding a white rat in its paws?
White lie is what we tell the boss
When we just want to stay indoors

White line is how Robbie got caught
Because it was still stuck to his nose
White gold is what I wear around my neck
Sometimes just for a pose

White pudding on my plate
So I had to turn it back
Whitewash is what you get
If your crickets really crap

White slavery was abolished
Women were set free
White goods from Dixon's and Curry's
No interest charge for me

Whitehall at the centre of Government
Where the Blair's live tax-free
White Supremacy will never rule the world
It can only affect you and me

CONCORDE

The world is set to move
At a slower pace
As Concorde gets ready
For its resting place

She shall no more
Grace our blue skies
As people look up
With a tear in their eyes

Her body so long
Yet so sleek
Travelling at Mach II
At sixty thousand feet

She first came to light in '69
This bird was definitely ahead of her time

Just over three hours to New York
You can leave here at ten
Then get to New York
And have coffee again

For thirty odd years
She's carried the rich
But now on their last time
One hundred was picked

They flew supersonic
Then they flew non-stop
Is this really the time
For this bird to rot?

Just one single flaw
She had in her time
That crash in 2000
That killed many lives

The way we spell Concorde
Was dictated by the French
They wouldn't accept it
Without an 'E' on the end

It's the end of an era
It's the end of an age
Will we ever see planes
Go this fast again?

PERIVALE GARAGE

Let's not forget why it took so long

They had to make sure Perivale was strong

With its new foundations

And the new recruits

Led by a team even Blair would choose

From this day forward lets make it the best

Be proud of ourselves

And the way that we dress

Cos Perivale Garage will be here for a while

Now that's a good reason to go home with a smile.

THE DEMONS WITHIN US

The Demons that sit within us
Make us do silly things

The Demons that never leave our minds
Can make us sink or swim

Some of us who survive those Demons
Can only thank God

But some of those who didn't make it
Lay still in the clouds above

The Demons comes in different forms
You would never tend to expect

Like the man that robs
And the man that steals
Can never command respect

The Demons can affect us all
Can make us mad or insane

Some of us it hits the wrong note
So we may never love again

The Demons can affect the good
But always touch the bad
To fight the Demons
You have to be strong
Don't let it make you feel sad

There's Demons that make us hate ourselves
Only the Demons can tell us why

They used a cross on Dracula
Then told him to open his eyes

Think positive things
And the Demons will go
'Cos it hates a happy mind
Channel your thoughts and think ahead
All good things come in time

THE WORD BLOOD

Blood that flows through our veins
Sometimes boil when enraged
Blood can run cold
When the feelings go numb
Bad blood is what you get
When you can't get along
Blood test to check
To see what's wrong
Blood group and blood type
Sing the very same song
Blood brothers go way back
No blood money can split
Bloodthirsty is how you feel
When a man dis your chick
Blood clart is you what you tell him
Bring the blood donor quick
Had a drink called Bloody Mary
Woke up feeling sick
Blood sports should be abolished
Maybe teach the fox new tricks
Put the bloodhounds into retirement
And teach them how to catch fish
Blood poisoning from the enemy
Revenge is my only wish
Blood pressure has to be stable
Bloodsucker is not a dish
Blood is thicker than water
Not a wivestale or even myth
Blood is found in all of us
Bloodstains can be removed with Dreft
Having blood on ones hands
Have two meanings to you and me
Going down to the blood bank
Just means joining the queue

WHAT THE PAPERS SAID

I just want to fly, fly through air
Across the Atlantic to even Bel Air
Meet Fresh and Prince
And tell them I care
And hope to God they pay my fare!

The money's for free if you know where
No time for puzzles or questionnaires
They tease your mind and waste your time
Some people like the way I rhyme
Sometimes it sucks some time it's fine
I can't perform every time

I sit here pondering my latest plan
Wouldn't it be funny if I met Saddam?
I would ask about the price of oil
Then ask about that chemical soil

Wouldn't it be funny if some people where poor
Like Michael Jackson and Barrymore
They would be locked up for the things they did
Like dangling their child and smoking a spliff

What about Norton
And the way he's so camp?
What about Lewis
I hear he's The Champ?

Even Jamie Oliver the way he cooks fish
Along with that accent he's taking the piss
Trevor Mc Donald who reads the news
Relaying the rubbish on Government views

What's the problem with Britney Spears
Snorting Cocaine through her ears?
These are the stories need not be aired
So give us some substance or disappear

Mugabe's in France seeing Jacques Le Worm
I wonder if he told how his people burned
Concorde returned with three engines running
The people on board thought their time was coming

Serena Williams shows her body to all
I bet she's never had a double fault called
Argos and Littlewoods have been fined for their scam
They wanted all Barbies to be turned into a man

Having a red nose is part of the fun
It's about that Charity that someone begun

If I had a plan I would sack the Mayor called Ken
For charging us a fiver to go in the West End
His has no car nor bike or friend
But plans for the charges to go up again

What about Robbie Williams for shagging those blondes?
He shagged them for the fun of it
Then took them to the Proms

What about Michael Douglas and Catherine Zeta Jones?
They got married the other day
One million set in stone

But who am I? Not Judge nor Jury
Put pen to paper to tell you this story

MY VALENTINE

For me to describe my Valentine
Not tears in your eyes, but only mine

We all know someone we really love
In war and peace and up above

So treat her special
Till the end of time

I pen this poem for my Valentine.

MICHAEL JACKSON

Who would have thought
Michael Jackson was Black
If you saw him today
You would say he was White

The things that he has done
To his skin and his face
It's hard to place him
In a particular race

He must be confused
From deep within
Check out the way
He has bleached his skin

We knew for a fact
He's The King of Pop
He's good at moon walking
And dancing in socks

He was the first artist
To wear a mask
Then came the glove
Now his kids wear a scarf

He loved all his animals
Including Bubbles The Chimp
He has his own Zoo
Where he keeps them all in

He got rid of Bubbles
Now he plays with his kids
What famous cartoon
Would he like to be in?

He loves all his family
And loves all his fans
He dreams one day
Of being Peter Pan

And now that his career
Seems to be going nowhere
Remember the day of the afro hair?

He sang some great songs
He sang some great hits
Remember that song
That thrilled us to bits?

He has these crazy moments
He does crazy things
But that is the way
Michael Jackson is

Sold many records
Went platinum back then
Will we ever see this man
Sing live again?

THAT WORD HEART

The Heart of the matter is
We have all had our Hearts broken
Whether losing a loved one
Or broken relationships
Missing the sales or that holiday trip

Heart stopping moments
As we watch that film
Take Rennie for that heartburn
You know it's the deal
Heartless people are everywhere
Have no conscience, they just don't care

Remember that programme called Heart to Heart?
The detective series that climbed up the charts
Heartbreak Hotel
That's what Michael sang
I cross my Heart as the funeral began

I remember at school and those Love Heart sweets
We had them at break time
We had them as treats

Some people don't hold back
And wear their Heart on their sleeves
While others have Heart attacks
Which bring them to their knees

There are people that are so kind
They have a Heart of gold
Then there are those that give us Heartache
They're sure to grow old alone.

The rich and the famous
Also known as Heartthrobs
Remember that scary man
From the Wizard of Oz?

If you want to give something be a Heart Donor
Could help someone live ten years longer
Have you ever played cards
And get the nine of Hearts?
Hand on my Heart,
I prefer darts

Such a simple word
With so many meanings
I end this passage
'Cos my Heart is bleeding

HURRICANE ISABEL

Don't mess with a hurricane
It will blow you away
Just ask the poor people of the U.S.A
It came from the Atlantic
And it came non-stop
Not even traffic lights
Could make the wind speed drop

Windows getting barred up
People start to leave town
I wonder who's insured with the district crown?

It batters the coastline
Then moves inland
I wonder if BUSH has an Emergency Plan?

Hope it's not the same plan he used in IRAQ
Cos there's gonna be eaten by a deep-sea shark
Her name was Isabel but this was no girl
She has a massive punch and even bigger twirl

People in the street
Couldn't stand upright
When the winds hit one hundred
Some get blown like a kite

Telegraph poles come crashing down
Forty foot waves that swallow a town
President Bush flees the Washington State
He heads for Camp David where his family's safe

People are told to write their names on forearms
The eye of the storm the most deadly so far
Rain lashing hard that it feels like sand
There's people that chase these storms across land

The last storm they had was in Ninety-Nine
Hurricane Floyd won the crown at the time
But along came Isabel and she showed what she got
If Floyd were around he would have surely got fucked.

WHY 2

Why does fuel cost so much?
Why does the English weather suck?
Why does a cat always land on its feet?
Why does my socks smell like cheese after a week?
Why does time stop for no man?
Why does the best electronics come from Japan?
Why do I have to wait so long in the queue?
Why do Mondays seem so blue?
Why do passengers ask me why?
Why do babies like to cry?
Why does my hairs sometimes stand on end?
Why did they call that clock Big Ben?
Why do people carry guns?
Why do women suddenly become nuns?
Why does sods law seem everywhere?
Why does Bush seem to control Blair?
Why does love sometimes hurt?
Why did they call this place planet Earth?
Why does rain seem to follow me?
Why do buses come in threes?
Why did the postman knock twice?
Why does the whole world eat rice?
Why is the air so thin in space?
Why did Michael do that to his face?
Why does money seem to go round?
Why does Lord Lucan need to be found?
Why does day turn into night?
Why do cats and dogs fight?
Why do tooth aches always hurt?
Why does sun cream stop you being burnt?
Why do politicians always lie?
Why does Gabriel wear a patch over her eye?
Why did Tyson take that tasty bite?

Why did Alliyah take that tragic flight?
Why does luck never come my way?
Why do Muslims pray five times a day?
Why does my cold seem to never go away?
Why did Nostradamos predict the future so well?
Why do schoolteachers all ways ring that bell?
We all know the answers to some of these questions
Don't ask me why I wrote this selection.

MIRRORS

A mirror reflects day
As well as reflecting light
A mirror reflects shadows
That makes you scared in the night

A mirror hangs there on the wall
Never seeing another room
Some mirrors travel in a bag
Some mirrors go to school

Some mirrors get to see the toilets
While girls fix their hair
While mirrors in the 'gents'
Gets smashed up by a chair

Some mirrors make you look so thin
While others make you look fat
Some mirrors have a mind of their own
Some mirrors even talk back

A mirror can bring the sun from outside
And bend it in the light
Add twenty more mirrors
You're onto winner
You'll be watching the day at night

Concave or convex
The type you may choose
By picking a small one
You just cannot lose

We find them on cars
In trains and in loo's
Some mirrors are broken
Some mirrors abused

Some mirrors tell lies
Some mirrors tell truths
Most of the time
It's there to amuse

But if they get broken
Seven years bad luck
Get one with a guarantee
That says it won't crack

CELEBRATIONS OF FAITH

Snow flakes drifting past the windowpane
Those cold dark nights are here again
As we celebrate Guy Fawkes
And light up the skies
Seven weeks from now
Out buying mince pies
From Christmas cakes, puddings and even nuts
It's always a joy to see the turkey stuffed
As families gather round
To exchange presents and gifts
And to think of all those people that they really miss
But it's not only Christmas celebrated by all
Diwali in London
Right down to Southall
A three-day event
Know as the Festival of Light
With the exchange of sweets
And fire works at night
Family and friends also gather round
To mark the New Year
And continue to be proud
Eid marks the end of Ramadan
You cannot eat or drink
When light shines on the land
A time to remember those
Who do not have enough to eat
Brings them closer to Allah
Makes them feel complete
Enjoy a dish called kaju katli
Full of cashew peanuts
Cannot be allergic to these
The Jews have a celebration
That takes place in midwinter
Channuka it is called

Was told by my friends sister
Dedication of the Holy Temple
After desecration by the Greeks
One candle is lit each night
Until eight makes it complete
Children receive gifts
And people eat traditional foods
Like doughnuts and fried potato latkes
Sounds delicious to me and you
As the year draws ever nearer
And celebrations continue on
Let's rid the world of poverty
Stop building the nuclear bomb.

VICTIMS OF WAR

Who said Hitler didn't shoot himself?
I know it wasn't me
I was nowhere near this planet Earth

Nostradamos had many predictions
Some folks back then thought it was fiction
But who would have thought many would come true
Take for example World War II

It lasted for years, and killed many
Tanks and guns
They fought two a penny
They conquered the French and Belgium's quick
They had no chance against the swastika stick

If you were black you know you would die
But if you're a Jew they gassed you so high

They don't give a damn
Just told many lies
The colour of your skin
Meant life or death

There's no point taking the acid test
They died by the gun or tortured slow
They pulled their fingers and little toes

Their screams of pain
Fell on deaf ears
They even started to kill them in pairs

If only he knew what really came true
He would dedicate that book to you

I am glad I wasn't living way back then
'Cos I wouldn't be holding this Parker Pen

SEPTEMBER 9/11

Looking over Manhattan
Where the Twin Towers once stood
The thought of that day
As it flashed across the news
While sitting at home
Watching it on TV
When a plan hit the side
Stood there and couldn't believe
There were screams and shouts
As the plane plunges to the streets
Bodies all broken
Some covered with sheets
I will never forget that day
Can't erase it from my mind
Especially when another plan
Hit the second Tower in line
As the cameras zoom in
People screaming for their lives
One hundred floors up
Some certain to die
People jumping from windows
In a futile attempt to escape
They're dead before they hit the ground
To their makers they will meet
We thought we had seen it all
With the Towers in a blaze
Then the first one started to crumble
Until it was totally raised
Before the dust had settled
The second Tower starts to fall
As the structure starts to give way
Cascading from floor to floor
I feel for the people trapped inside
Some can't be saved at all
This was not an act of God
For the plans were flown by men
Their destiny lies high above
As terrorists we condemn.

FORGOT ABOUT GEE?

Some people say I've been missing
But they don't seem to realise
That I've been sitting in a dark room
Just writing up these few lines
So fuck those who thought I was dead
Now they see me on stage
Now they want to be my friend
They want me to flex with them again
But I am taking a step forward
I won't be taking a step back
So you can stay there with your crummy lives
And smoking up the crack
I am not down with it no more
I am not down like Dirty Den
Some of those who think I have money
You better stop and think again
Where the fuck was you when my bills were due?
Answer phone machine on again
Now you see me on the TV screen
Now you want to be my friend?
Sometimes I want to scream and shout
I am not gonna try and pretend
On those cold and dark and lonely nights
While I am driving in my Benz
Hitting the freeway at over a hundred miles
Getting chased by the cops again
I don't think I am gonna slow down
Because the needle says 'two ten'
I got nine points on my license
Don't need to be stopped again
Where I go from here only God really knows
Because he's my best friend
What's the point of being on this planet?
If you don't even have a dream?
It's dreams that fuel our minds
I want a bigger, faster machine
I've met traitors, I've met liars
I've met those who try and deceive

I've met niggers who want a piece of the cake
But don't even know how to say please.
To catch a mouse in the kitchen
You have to tempt him out with the cheese
When Tyson fought Lennox Lewis
He got chopped down like a tree
Now he stays in his room at night
I hear he's just history
I got friends who died at twenty-one
But none at forty-three
When it's time to take your ass above
You got to let it be
Don't believe the hype
That you will be back
Maybe even bigger than me
Check out those who died in 64 and those in 63?
If you think they're gonna come back
What do you think they will come back to be?
Could be a house could be a car
Or even a big bag of weed
If it's that they will just get rolled up
And blown out to sea
If I was to ever come back
I would come back as me
These lyrics they could have been written
While I was still in my teens
Whilst sitting in the classroom
I'll be part of history
Not the Saxons not the Romans
But me just being me
I've never claimed to be a writer
That's why I am writing this for free
But there are those out there
With their hands stretched out
Looking for something big from me
Who the hell do they think I am?
I am no Ayatollah or Prophet
Every time I get my paycheck
It's not what I expect it to be
I am not talking dollars, dimes or cents
It's the minimum wage for me

I am not crazy, I am not foolish
I can't be what you want me to be

CHANGES

As I sit here watching the day go by
I know I gotta hold my head up high
Things ain't what they seem to be
I think I am living in a distant dream
Where the money's free and the cops don't bother me
Stop knocking at my door at four and three
Got a message from the Man above
Only care about those who I truly love
There's those that passed away
Just give a thought
They're never gonna see this day
The power of thought can keep you sane
When shown no love
No it's not the way
Oh God can you feel my pain
As I crumble inside and I melt away
Can you feel my spark it's a slow decay
The thought of dying would be a crying shame
Not to see the light or my nephews play
Brings tears to my eyes
So I walk away
One shot to the head could have ended my day
That's one kind of lottery
I refuse to play
I feel for my brothers down in Africa
All the poor people down in Somalia
I wish I could do something for all of ya
Bring the rain down and make things grown for ya
Make the rivers flow so the seeds can grow
And the children will grow up to know that I know
That this isn't the way it's supposed to go
Lets hold a petition to let the whole world know
That they're living large and living fat
Whilst these starving children, no clothes on their backs
Never seen an email or sent a fax
Never held a mobile or drank water from a tap
But isn't it time we gave something back?
Instead of killing each other and watching our backs

Those guns worth less than an average snack
They were bought by the Government to make us attack
But what do you do when you're a victim too?
And the whole world takes no notice of you
But what can I say? Bought a gun today
Stop my family being victims of this latest craze
If only I could make things better for you
The Pope, The President and Biggie too,
I would bring back Tupac and we could roll as a crew
We would act like idols like you're supposed to do
The Pope would preach about this and that
How to be good children and stay off the crack
Biggie and Tupac would be best friends
Those drive-by shootings would come to an end
And what about The President I hear you say?
Has Nuclear Bombs for a rainy day
Or is this to protect the American Way?
And will I need a Visa to come and stay?
What the hell is going on in the world today?
When our kids are not safe from the Internet preys?
The planet's red hot from space it's a glaze
War Number Three could be a matter of days
The race is on to reach the planet Mars
It seems so safe in the distant stars
One push of a button, time for Doomsday
Mushroom clouds drifting in the Milky Way

BEING ALONE

Try to understand
How loneliness feels
When no one rings your phone
Or invite you to meals
People all around but nobody cares
That man in the room
No visitors for years
It's a soul-searching thing
When you feel all alone
There's family that love you
But don't really know
The hours seem like days
As time drifts slowly by
One day felt so low
And started to cry
Can you hear what I am saying?
Do you know where I am coming from?
You could know a hundred people
But still feel alone
People see you smiling
But can't read the lines
A man in a mask
Who's crying inside
Someone that misses you and tells you so
Can make you feel high
When feeling so low
Those little phone calls
Telling you that they care
Worth more than gold to the lonely out there
It's said that time's a great healer
How come I am still in tears?
This room feels so cold
With no one to share
So much time to think
With the mind in despair
Those cold lonely nights
Sometimes hard to bear
As the walls get ever closer

Transfixed in a stare
The thought of ending it all
Just doesn't compare
As the sunset lowers
Beneath the distant roof tops
Its time to start again
It's time to move on.

THE MOBILE PHONE

When mobiles first came out
They were as big as a house
Fifteen years later they're as small as a mouse

To carry one then
Was bit of a sight
Most people thought it was a weapon to fight

The standby time lasted only two calls
Had to put it on charge
Had to wait for a pause

The reception wasn't great
But the idea fun
Some thought it was a telly
Where's BBC1?

As years have gone by
Things start to get smaller
With Erickson, Sony and even Motorola

The things that they do
Would amaze back then
The size of some phones
Is the size of some pens

They email and fax
And send pictures too
The even have phones
That fit in a shoe

But four different networks
To chose for a call
No telephone boxes
No standing outdoors

The Japs' have a phone
That sits on your wrist

You can even watch telly
While taking a piss

It started with a string
And then a few cans
Now they have phones
That fit in a van

No need to drive
With a phone at your ear
They have something called 'hands-free'
That'll leave you to steer

You receive a call
From around the world
You can even ring back
All that credit to burn

Now that the phones
Can fit in a bag
Some still have those big phones
I think it's real sad

How small can they get?
Only time will tell
I think they have phones
You can even smell

The phone was one of those great inventions
I got mine
What's your intention?

ADJUSTING THE CLOCKS

Another day in London
Just doesn't seem fun
Raindrops lashing down
I think summers begun

The time is now April
Saw the back of March
Those long and dark days
Is now a thing of the past

The T-shirts are out
But so are the umbrellas
What happened to the sunshine?
They forgot to tell us
We wait in vain for the clouds to clear
Get rid of those boots
And knitted underwear

The clocks went forward
Like we controlled time
Go see the movie, 'Matrix'
To get this rhythm

The rain's slowing down
Clouds starting to disperse
Put hand to heart as I watch a hearse

The umbrellas close as the sun comes out
The brighter it gets the bigger the crowd
The roofs are off on those big shiny cars
No wonder they're feeling like superstars

Don't have to drive fast just drive really slow
With the price of fuel, five miles to go
The parks are full with people at play
Like swimming and jogging and chatting away

Only four months of summer that's what we have left

Before it gets dark let's start to invest
Who gave us the power to control the time?
Let's change it back then set it to nine

Why is the word abbreviation written so long?
Compared to our summer it seems like a song
When the clocks go back we know it's the end
Waiting for summer to restart again

CATS

They're fluffy and cute
And as small as a ball
They start out as kittens
In a litter of four
Their mouths barely open
And eyes not at all

Some sit down and play
Some just like to crawl
Chase anything that moves
Scratch anything that don't

They sit in your lap for hours on end
They like to be stroked
They're always your friend
They jump over fences
And climb up the trees
They roll in the sunshine
Some take in the breeze

With razor sharp claws
For scratching those doors
A cat has no hands
But tiny soft paws
They land on their feet
And never on their back
They have nine lives
Which we humans lack

Cats are forever
And not for Christmastime
They're not a bunch of roses
You just give to your wife

With big sparkling eyes
They can see clear at night
With sensitive ears
They hear the smallest mite

They're named after people
And named after friends
Like Penny and Simba
And that Ginger called Benz
They even have names like Bonnie and Clyde
Remember those Gangsters from '45?
Some die on the crossroads
Some die of old age
How can we forget the fun that they gave?

DANCING PANDA

In June I saw
A Panda
Dancing for some food

Dancing, rolling
Jumping, dropping
But the keeper gave no food

Panda burning through
The summer heat
Not surviving with
It's feet

Children laughing at
The creature, but
Did not see the burning eyes
But saw laughter and comedy

The laughter had just then stopped
And all around their
Hearts felt sorrow
By watching an ungrateful plot.

By Myles Costello, aged 10

CHEW ON THIS

Life is full of its twists and turns
In relations and love
We all have to learn

To show our love to our fellow man
Were not all the same must understand

All colours and creeds must all unite
Along with the battle
We may have to fight

Catholics and Protestants may never get on
Always show by example let's all be strong

India and Pakistan have nuclear bombs
They point across borders
Yet pray to one God

Too many Countries with bombs at each others throats
Just takes one button to send us in smoke

The hatred and seething across the world
With children dying and adults burn

The beatings and killings double every day
More than that train crash I am sad to say

The effects of one country
Can affect us all
Makes no difference if rich or poor
We must all try and have some fun
Before the whole world becomes a big mushroom

If we could find how to live as one
There would be no need for a Nuclear Bomb
But life in itself is no bed of roses
We must try and not get up each other's noses.

THE CLOCK INSIDE

Standing starring through those
Big black gates
Tombstones standing high
For this is the place
Where time stands still
All bodies facing up to the sky

Daffodil wreaths
Wither and decay
Graves without any stone
No name, no honor, no title
Sometimes called the unknown

As the last rites are read
Everything that could be said was said
Now it's time to bury the dead

As the meek shall inherit the Earth
Just as Christ was breading the Bread
Nothing in life is ever certain
Only that one day we will all be dead

Ashes to Ashes
Dust to dust
Only in God, we put our trust
When it's time to go
Only you will know
For the message will come from above

As life flashes by
Like the speed of a gun
So short and sometimes unreal
Our time on the Earth
Has already been written
Like the Bible, the Koran
Can you feel?

No one lives forever

Sometimes hard to digest
The clock inside is slowing
Keeps ticking until the end.

WHEN I'M GONE

When I'm gone
Have a drink on me
Don't be sad because I'm free
Free from the challenges of daily life
Of broken hearts and tearful nights
When I'm gone
Turn the music up
Put that tune on that makes you jump
When I'm gone
The world moves on
It stops for no man
Weak or strong
When I'm gone
Don't lose no sleep
Sleep makes you feel energized
Every day of the week
When I'm gone
Don't shed no tears
I'm just a mere mortal
Who's run out of years
When I'm gone
Don't be mad
Think of all the memories
We all shared and had
When I'm gone
I want a smile on my face
The smile that I had
When I played kiss chase
When I'm gone
I don't want to go with the wind
Lay me in the earth
In a simple coffin
When I'm gone
Let the sun warm your days
As if I was there
In a cloud or a haze
When I'm gone
I want the world to know

I was 'ere
Didn't make a million
But found someone who cared
When I'm gone
What ever is mine is yours
Forgive and forget
It could open closed doors.

At last the hard work is done. The road has been long, bumpy and winding. Battles of the mind fought and lost along the way. I had a dream to see my work in print and I want to say to those who believed in me, who inspired and motivated me, Thank you. Your words of inspiration were truly needed in my darkest hours.

The poems that I have written depict events and topics, which have been experienced, seen and heard. Some reflect my innermost thoughts, our daily lives and the issues faced by our global community. I hope that you have read something, which you can relate to. I hope that, in some way, you have been touched.

I would also like to thank Myles Costello, aged ten years, for his excellent contribution and hope it inspires him to write many more, well done.

Enjoy.

GARY CHRISTOPHER
May 2005

Printed in the United Kingdom
by Lightning Source UK Ltd.
107006UKS00001B/139-183

9 781420 868647